THE CAMINO REAL
(The King's Road)
Activity Book

Spanish Settlers in the Southwest

Walter D. Yoder, Ph.D.

SUNSTONE PRESS

Santa Fe
New Mexico

IN APPRECIATION

Sunstone Press is grateful to Gaea McGahee, Museum Educator;
John Cabrera, Co-Chair, Museum School Outreach Program; and
Ann Mahar Co-Chair, Museum School Outreach Program of the New Mexico State University
Museum in Las Cruces, New Mexico for their many corrections and suggestions for this edition.

Revised edition

ISBN: 0-86534-218-0

Published by Sunstone Press • Post Office Box 2321
Santa Fe, New Mexico 87504-2321 / USA
(505) 988-4418 / FAX: (505) 988-1025
orders only (800) 243-5644

The CAMINO REAL
(The King's Road)
Activity Book

This book is about the history of the Camino Real. This trade route threads through the arid regions of Northern Old Mexico and into the modern state of New Mexico. The trail was over twelve hundred miles long. Wagons drawn by horses, mules, and oxen took many weeks to travel the entire length from Mexico City to Santa Fe in the territory of New Mexico. This was a great adventure involving the excitement and dangers of nature and often, encounters with native peoples. Stretches of waterless deserts, vast sand dunes, rocky trails, and deep canyons made progress slow. Only people with strong bodies and character could make the journey.

The trail brought together three colorful and exciting cultures. the Hispanic traders pioneers originating from Spain and Old Mexico, Anglo traders from Europe and the Eastern part of the United States, and Native Americans who were the original inhabitants of the Americas.

Trade and profit were the main reasons these early pioneers and traders came so far. People along the way were eager to buy and trade for articles of every description. Fabrics, tools, animal skins, and all kinds of hardware were hauled by wagon and pack animals along the trail. The rural farmers of the southwest were dependent on the Camino Real as a way to get their crops to market.

The activities in this book will help you to understand these dangers, excitement and rewards experienced by the people traveling on the Camino Real. The American Southwest developed rapidly with the arrival of these early pioneers.

The First Europeans

The **Camino Real** (the King's Road) was first traced through the Southwest by the Spanish Conquistadores. Looking for gold, these early adventurers followed trails used by the original Native Americans. These soldiers had special weapons and equipment for protection. Match the names of each with the corresponding numbers in the illustration.

Turn the page upside down to discover the correct answers.

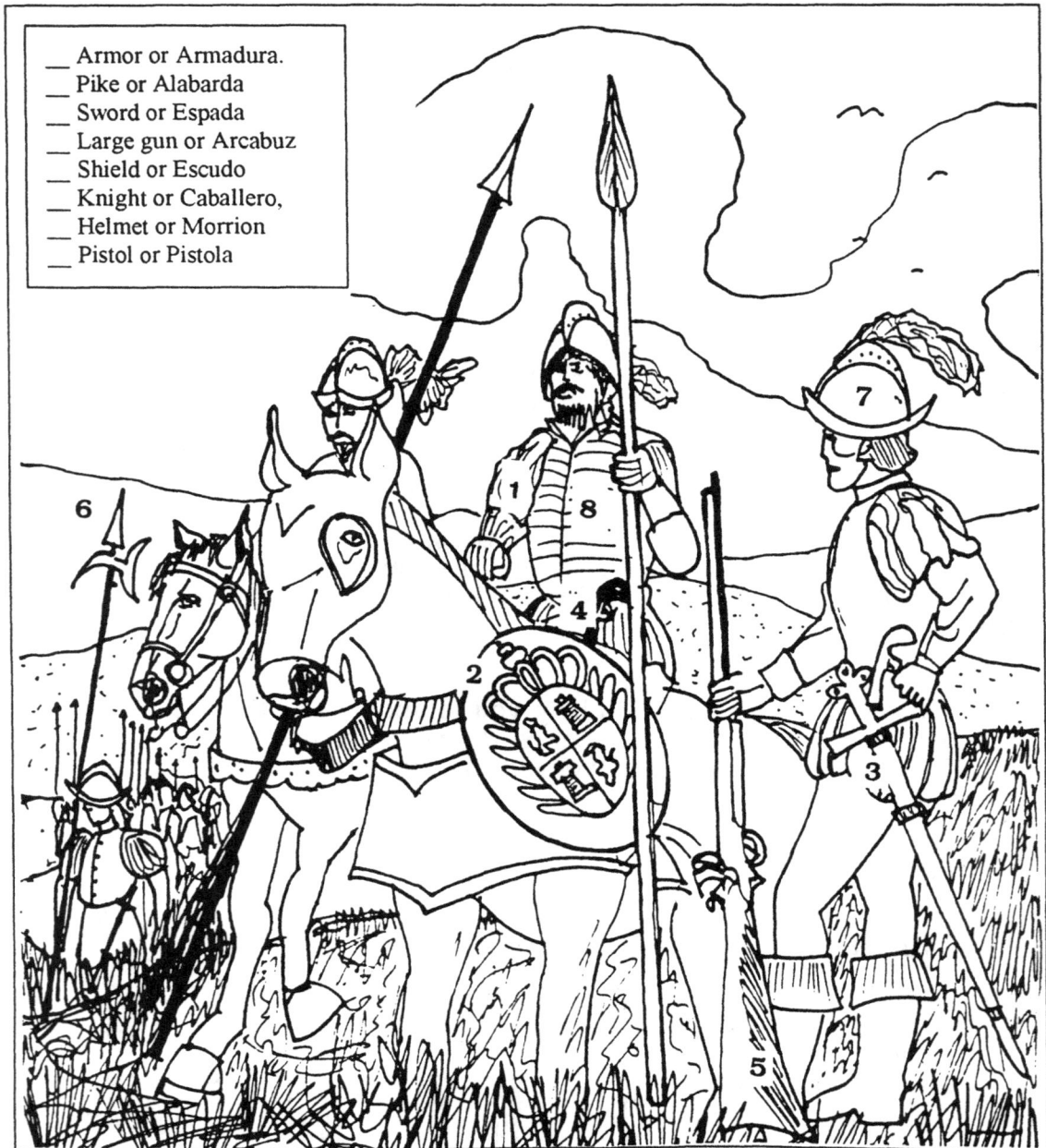

___ Armor or Armadura.
___ Pike or Alabarda
___ Sword or Espada
___ Large gun or Arcabuz
___ Shield or Escudo
___ Knight or Caballero,
___ Helmet or Morrion
___ Pistol or Pistola

1) Knight or Caballero, 2) Shield or Escudo, 3) Sword or Espada 4) Pistol or Pistola, 5) Large gun or Arcabuz, 6) Pike or Alabarda, 7) Helmut or Morrion, 8) Armor or Armadura.

Where is the Camino Real (The King's Highway) ?

The Camino Real joined the Santa Fe Trail at Santa Fe, New Mexico. This city is marked with a star on the map below. Identify these trails by tracing the route of the Camino Real in red and the Santa Fe Trail in blue. Unscramble the names of all the modern states and countries on the map. Write the correct spelling of each on the lines provided.

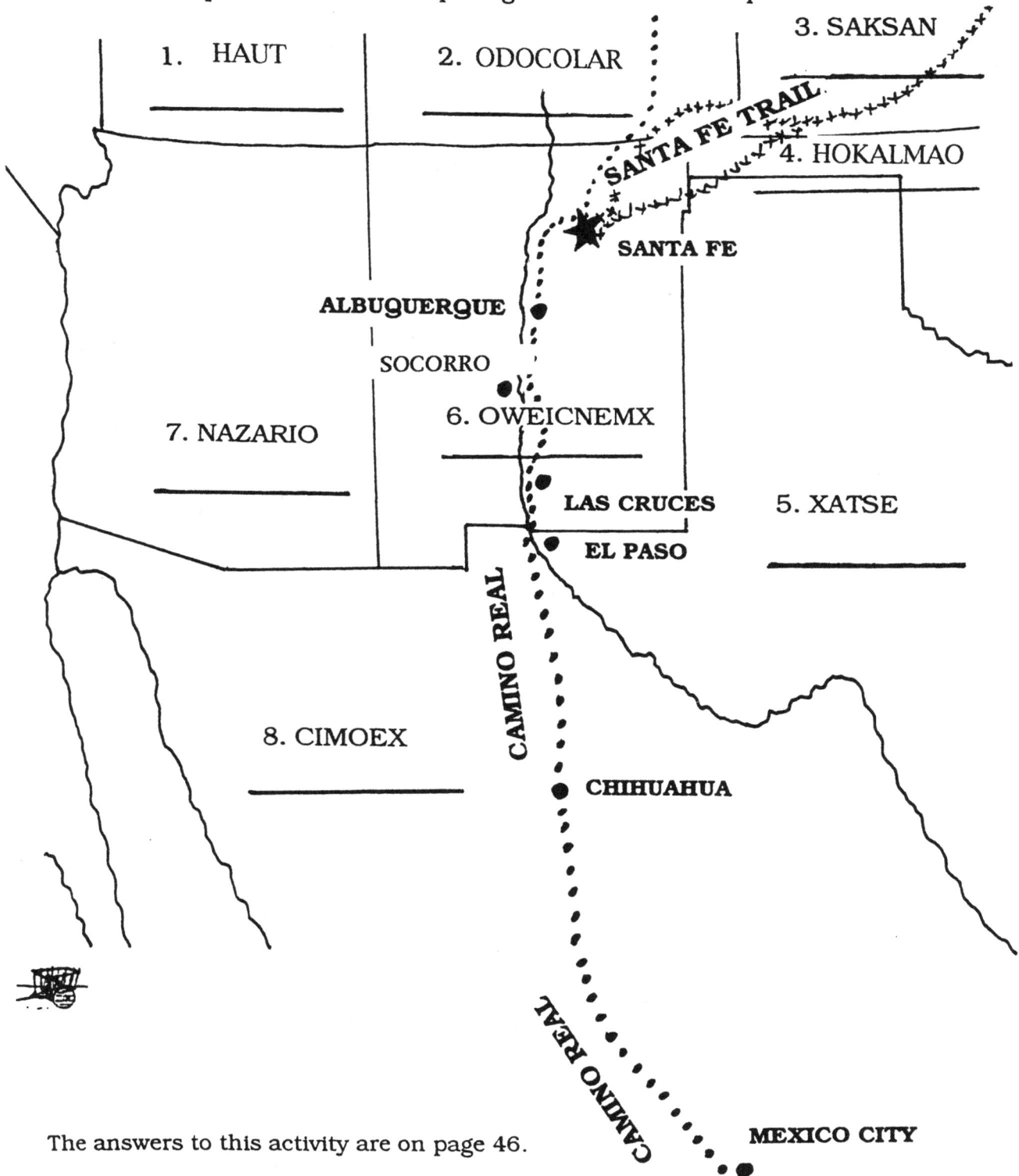

1. HAUT
_____

2. ODOCOLAR
_____

3. SAKSAN
_____

4. HOKALMAO
_____

5. XATSE
_____

6. OWEICNEMX
_____

7. NAZARIO
_____

8. CIMOEX
_____

SANTA FE TRAIL

SANTA FE

ALBUQUERQUE

SOCORRO

LAS CRUCES

EL PASO

CAMINO REAL

CHIHUAHUA

CAMINO REAL

MEXICO CITY

The answers to this activity are on page 46.

THE CAMINO REAL IN NEW MEXICO

29. EL Paso Del Norte   VILLA

28. La Salinera_____

27. Los Brazitos_____

26. Dona Ana_____

25. Robledo_____

24. San Diego_____

23. Ojo del Perrillo_____

22. La Cruz del Aleman_____

21. Ojo_____

20. Fray Christobal_____

19. Valverde_____

18. Luis Lopez_____

17. Socorro_____

16. La Joya de Sevilleta_____

15. Felipe Romero_____

14. Las Nutrias_____

13. Casa Colorada_____

12. Tomé_____

11. Valencia_____

10. Peralta_____

9. Isleta_____

8. Albuquerque_____

7. Alameda_____

6. Sandia_____

5. Bernalillo_____

4. Algodones_____

3. SanFelipe_____

2. Santo Domingo__

1. Santa Fe_____

RIO GRANDE RIVER

SANTA FE TRAIL

CAMINO REAL

Until the early 1800s most trade in New Mexico came up the Rio Grande Valley on the Camino Real. Many places or stops developed along the way such as villas, towns, haciendas, camps, and springs. All of these localities played an important role in the life of early New Mexico. Check the key and determine what type of locality each stop represents and complete the list by putting the correct symbol by each locality.

KEY TO MAP SYMBOLS

Villa (chartered town)

Pueblo (town)

Hacienda (ranch)

Paraje (camp)

Mesa or mountain

Camino Real · · · · · · · · · ·

Santa Fe Trail _____

Consult a current road map of New Mexico to determine which of these early stops on the Camino Real still exist.

The Camino Real Word Search

Listed below are several important words that you will notice as you read more about the Camino Real. Each word is given in Spanish and English. Find all of the words in Spanish in the word search diagram. These words can be horizontal, vertical, diagonal, or even backwards so look carefully for each one.

```
M A A L C A L D E D L A M A D R E A C E Q U I A
U A T Z O L U V W X Y Z R O L Z H O V P X U E L
L K E M A X S O N A C I R E M A S O L M O A M T
E L R P L O Z H Z M N E L M E R C A D O Q R R Z
R M R S I T S S A U Q S Z P Y O X Y S G P R V W
A P A R E J O T L P W T Y A U V B S T R T I L O
O N C P R H L Y E Z X A X W T N U F Q F S E N T
M V L Q E P E T A T E M A G Z H Y I J R K R J M
P L O J A T A V I X O P R E S I D I O E M O K P
A U T D S D Q G R V N I E F M A L I J L G N Q L
U C V A E N F R R M O D Y N C L X K K D I E L O
B V F W E C P J E R G A B O C A R N E S E C A S
V T T D H B V L O Z H N A Z S W R V C P D H S N
L G E X Y E B A S A X Y C D D I U G F F B O N U
W W S S K C L B M Z O V V A C R E T A Q G O U E
H R C T Z R A Q R O R E L O B I C E N F L G E V
X X O N B S M P S N S X C Y X B R S D Q H P V O
O Q P Y D R P M R A N C H O Z D E I A T K L M M
M E E O P I Q O T L U V W A E Q J N N J U V E E
U L T I M A T H U L E U B F C N E F G H I H J X
Y F A G V T P Q N G M T L S K R J D O G X I I I
T I E R R A I N C O G N I T A T A G Z H A M C C
C M N H R I Y N Z O A P C Q A R C Y I A Z L A A
L V S J P M N G H E O Z O B A L A C E J B N N O
Z K K W L H X K U I V D S B T B L A C K D O O O
A D B L I J F W J A X Z Y S Z R E Q L O P C S S
```

1. Calabozo - Jail
2. Jacal - a shanty
3. Los Americanos - Americans
4. Los Nuevomexicanos - New Mexicans
5. carne seca - dried meat
6. presido - fort
7. riata - noose
8. la madre acequia - the main ditch
9. tierra incognita - unknown land
10. Ultima thule - northern most point (Latin phrase)
11. fandango - party
12. carga - load
13. rico - rich person
14. escopeta - flintlock rifle
15. cibolero - buffalo hunter
16. el mercado - market place
17. estampida - stampede
18. rancho - ranch
19. llano - plain
20. vamos - lets go
21. sabe - understand
22. alcalde - mayor
23. carreta - cart
24. jerga - blanket
25. atajo - mule train
26. arrievo - mule driver
27. petate - mat
28. zalea - sheepskin
29. aparejo - pack saddle
30. mulera - bell mare

The solution to this activity is on page 46.

The Camino Real " Words to Know " Scramble

Camino Real

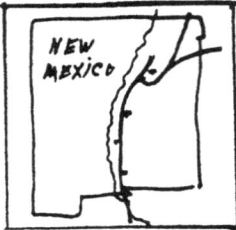

The King's Road. Starting at Mexico City, it provided a route through Mexico and New Mexico as far north as Santa Fe and Taos. Trails extended it into Colorado.

Parajes

This was the site of a temporary encampment on the Camino Real. Many Parajes became towns which still exist in New Mexico along the Camino Real.

Bosque

This is a narrow forest along the Rio Grande River. They are havens for wild animals and birds. Bosques provided shelter, water, and safety to Camino Real travelers.

Desierto

A Spanish term for the arid desert of the Southwest. Careful planning was necessary to cross stretches of the Camino Real. One area was called the " Jornada del Muerto " or the " Journey of the Dead Man "

Carreta

A two wheeled cart used to transport goods on the Camino Real. Some were very large and required several pairs of oxen to operate. The wheels were made of solid wood. Animal fat was used to lubricate the axle.

Presidio

A site on which a fort was built for protection. Some presidios became modern towns and cities along the Camino Real. Santa Fe and Albuquerque were presidios

Torreón

This is a tower made of logs, adobe, and stones. Torreones were usually built next to farms and towns for protection. Ruins of these towers can be found across the Southwest from Texas to California.

Caballo

This is Spanish for horse. The horse was brought to the Southwest by Spanish settlers and soldiers. Native Americans quickly captured the horse and used these animals to hunt and create raiding parties.

Arriero

This was the man that is in charge of the Atajo or wagon train. Mules were used to transport goods on the rock trails. Arrieros made the Camino Real a commercial success from the very start.

Atajo

This was the name for the long line of mules, pack horses or carretas that comprised a trading expedition. Many atajos made the journey along the Camino Real and the Santa Fe trail.

Unscramble the " Words to Know " Spell the word correcly in the space provided.

ELARNAIMOC
_____

AALLBOC
_____

RROONET
_____

RIDIOSEP
_____

AAJTO
_____

SOQEUB
_____

RORIRAE
_____

JAPSREA
_____

TISOREDE
_____

RARTECA
_____

Loading a " Mula de Carga " mule

A properly loaded mule insured that the animal would cooperate and carry the heavy load. If the load was too heavy or improperly balanced the mule would kick and grumble loudly. A blindfold was used on many animals to make the loading quicker and easier. The **Cargador** loaded the mule with the help of an assistant. The **Arriero** or mule driver led the **Atajo** or mule train down the trail.

Listed below are items used to load a mule. Put them in the order in which they were used. Place the appropriate numbers in the spaces provided. Check the picture to complete this activity.

A. Aparejo, the X shaped saddle,_____. B. Tapaojas, the blindfold,_____..
C. The Jerga, a woven saddle cloth,_____. D. The Zalea, a thick sheepskin used to protect the mule's back,_____. E. The cinch, a woven strap used to tighten down the load,_____.

The answers to this activity are on page 46.

A Mule Train on the Camino Real

Use desert colors to complete this illustration

The sure footed mule was used frequently on the trail to Old Mexico from Santa Fe. There were several natural barriers which allowed big cargo wagons to go only short distances. As trade increased the road was improved for large carretas and wagons. From the start, mule trains proved to be the most practical way of transporting goods over the Camino Real.

The three most Formidable barriers to travel on the Camino Real were:

1. The Bolsón de Mapimí, 2. The Bocas de los Médanos, and 3. The Jornada del Muerto.

Can you guess what these barriers were? After you look up the answers on page 46, locate these items on a modern map of Mexico and the United states.

The Mission at Doña Ana, New Mexico

A Stone and Adobe Church to Color

The village of Doña Ana began as a **Paraje** on the Camino Real. It is one of the first settlements in Southern New Mexico. This old mission is on the list of the National Register of Historic Places.

What is a Paraje? _____

The answer to this question is on page 46.

Safe Travel on the Camino Real

South of Santa Fe the route of the Camino Real went through the tribal lands of the Mountain Apache. In order to make the trip safely a military escort was often used to protect the slow moving wagons. Listed below are items which were needed to support a military escort. Friendly Native Americans were sometimes hired to help protect the Camino Real wagon trains. There are five items in the list that do not belong there. Find each one and explain why they are mistakes.

Firearms
Frozen vegetables
Gun powder
Lead shot
Bows
Arrows
Shields
Horses
Cannon
Dried meat
Radios
Dried corn
Beans
Live sheep
Live cattle
Electric razors
Water barrels
Dried peas
Bread
Canned fruit
Ice cream

Put the items that do not belong on this list in the blank spaces below.
1._____ 2._____ 3._____ 4._____ 5._____

Some interesting trail facts.

Supplies needed to operate a unit of eight Conestoga Wagons
320 yards of onesburg canvas for wagon covers

16 axes	500 pounds of tallow
24 pounds of heavy cord	150 wheel spokes
24 iron rims	48 first team mules
48 second team mules	8 heavy sledge hammers

Each wagon would also require an ample supply of nails, bolts, washers, pins, cleats, linchpins, ribs, crowbars, and ammunition.

The answers to this activity can be found on page 46.

The Spanish Soldiers are Coming

A historical rock picture to enlarge by the grid method.

Put the same lines in the small squares below in the corresponding squares in the empty grid on the next page.

Top

Bottom

Petroglyphs are pictures carved into large flat rocks by ancient peoples. They are of great historical value and should not be defaced or destroyed. This petroglyph shows Spanish soldiers on their way to the land of the pueblos approximately four hundred years ago. Circle the date below which best represents the real date so long ago.

1. 1930 a.d.   2. 1400 a.d.   3. 1600 b.c.   4. 1783 a.d.   5. 1890 a.d.   6. 1590 a.d.   7. 1000 b.c.

The answer to this question can be found on page 46.

Complete this grid picture by using shades of brown, tan, black, and other earth colors. You can use this grid technique to make other pictures larger or smaller. Be sure that the empty grid has exactly the same number of squares as the number of squares you put in the picture you are going to copy.

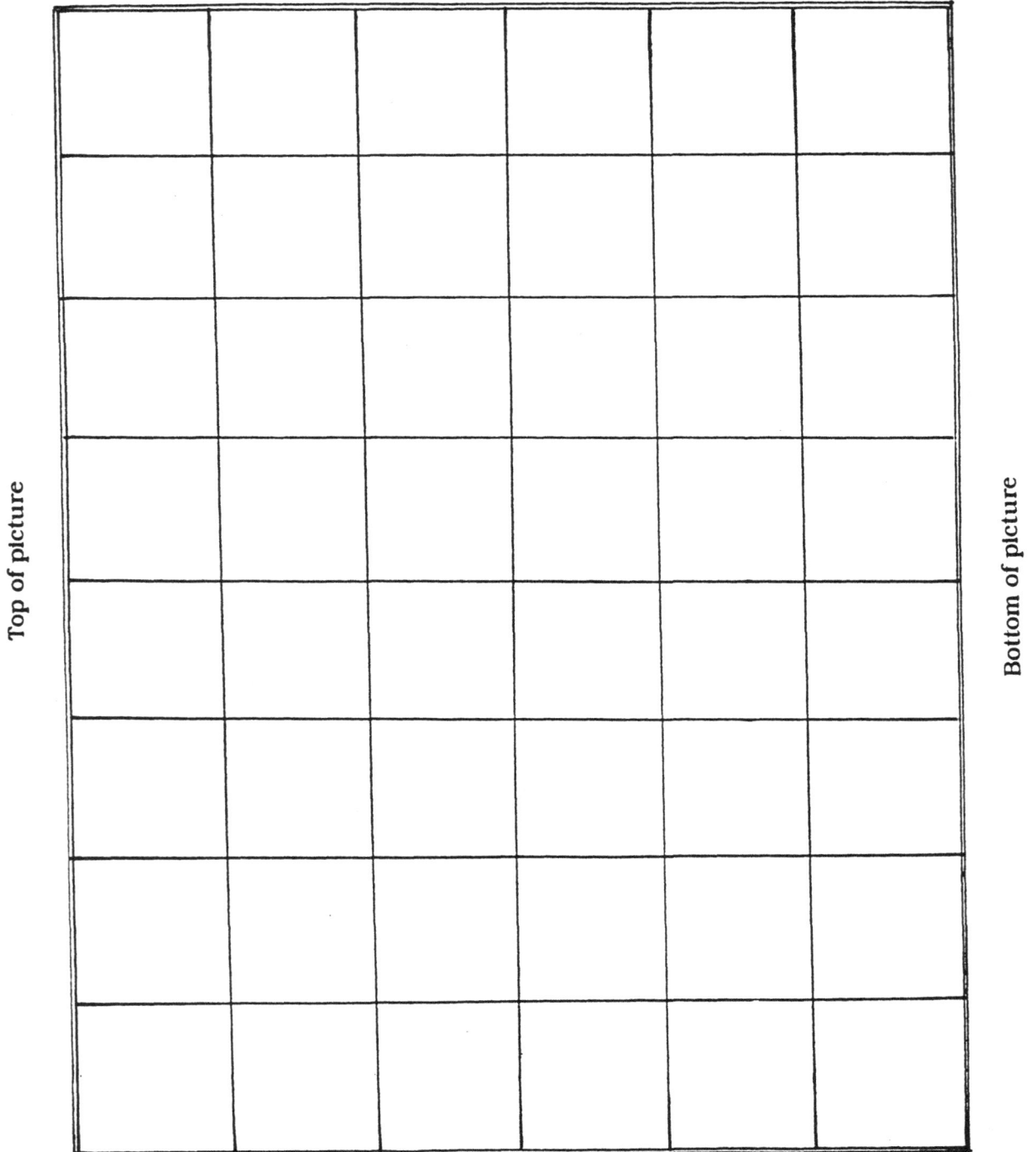

Top of picture

Bottom of picture

A Native American Petroglyph to Color

Trade Goods on the Camino Real

Mexico City, Mexico was at the southern end of the Camino Real. Most mule and wagon trains coming from New Mexico were assembled at Chihuahua which is 250 miles from El Paso, Texas, 580 miles from Santa Fe, New Mexico, and 1350 miles from Independence, Missouri. Below are two lists of trade goods which were pulled by mule, horse and oxen along the Camino Real. Can you figure out which list of items was taken north to Santa Fe and which group of trade goods was carried south to Old Mexico?

List number one	List number two
Woolen dress fabric	Metal tools
Woolen drapes	Fire arms
Wall hangings	Silk fabrics
Blankets	Boots
Cushions	Shoes
Over shirts	Sugar
Doublets	Black pepper
Jackets	Chocolate
Buffalo hides	Tobacco
Antelope hides	Liquors
Deer skins	Paper
Candles	Ink
Salt	Books
Pine nuts	Religious articles
El Paso wine	Toledo steel swords

Put the correct number next to the appropriate list.

#_____ are goods bound for Old Mexico.

#_____ are goods bound for Santa Fe.

The answers to this activity can be found on page 46.

Camino Real Mystery Object

A dot-to-dot project

This mystery object was built in many early Spanish settlements in New Mexico to protect farmers and villagers from hostile attack. What were the small squares holes used for? Also seen in this illustration is a beehive shaped Horno for baking bread, a Carreta for transporting heavy loads, and a Ramada to create shade for people and animals. Notice that the cart's wheels are made of solid wood.

The answer to this mystery is on page 46.

A mystery scene to solve

Our mystery scene has been cut and scattered into thirty squares. Draw the lines and images in each square into the same numbered square on the grid on the next page. Take your time and discover the mystery object.

The adobe church at Ranchos de Taos

This is one of the most famous adobe buildings in the world. Many artists have painted it. In this snowy scene, **luminarias** have been set out for Christmas Eve.

1	2	3	4	5
6	7	8	9	10
11	12	13	14	15
16	17	18	19	20
21	22	23	24	25
26	27	28	29	30

After you have reassembled the thirty squares, complete this holiday scene by using shades of tan, brown, and white. The sky in New Mexico is extremely blue because of the clean air and high altitude.

The Camino Real "Words to Know"

Decoding Game
These Words are in Spanish

Here are twelve "Words to Know" that will help you share the excitement of the Camino Real with your friends. Using the decoding chart at the bottom of the page, find the correct letter for each number to discover the answers to these questions.

1. This is the name given to the first Spanish explorers that brought the horse to the New World and discovered the Pueblos.
12,15,19 -3,15,14,17,21,9,20,1,4,15,18,5,19_____

2. This is the name given to the main water channel dug to irrigate the fields along the Rio Grande.
12,1-1,3,5,17,21,9,1-4,18,5_____

3. This is what people were called that hunted buffalo.
12,15,19-,3,9,2,15,12,5,18,15,19_____

4. These people were needed to translate Spanish into English for persons traveling along the Camino Real.
1-20,18,1,4,21,20,21,18_____

5. This is the name of the official piece of paper needed to travel on the Camino Real before the American occupation of New Mexico.
12,15,19-7,21,9,1,19_____

6. This is the Spanish term for the people that live in New Mexico.
12,15,19-14,21,5,22,15,13,5,24,9,3,1,14,15,19_____

7. This is what the men were called who were in charge of a mule train on the Camino Real.
12,15,19,-1,18,18,9,5,18,15,19_____

8. This is the name of a jail in Old Santa Fe.
5,12,-1,12,1,2,15,26,15_____

9. This is the term for the goods that were hauled by mule, oxen and horse on the Camino Real.
12,1-,3,1,18,7,1_____

10. This is the Spanish name for the people who were coming to New Mexico from the United States.
12,15,19-1,13,5,18,9,3,1,14,15,19_____

11. This is the name for the frequent parties that were held in Old Santa Fe in the old territorial days.
5,12,-6,1,14,4,1,14,7,15_____

12. This is what a Spanish lasso is called.
12,1-18,9,1,20,1_____

The Camino Real Time Line

Listed below are twelve dates and events that are important to the historical development of the Camino Real, later to be known as the Chihuahua Trail. Study the list carefully and put each item in its correct historical order starting with the earliest event. Space for this activity is at the bottom of the page.

1. **1912** - New Mexico becomes the 47th state to enter the Union.

2. **1862** - A Confederate Army under the command of General H. Sibley briefly occupies Santa Fe.

3. **1822** - The first wagon train carries trade goods to Santa Fe.

4. **1707** - Comanche and Ute Native Americans visit Santa Fe to make a peace treaty which will soon be broken.

5. **1880** - The construction of the Santa Fe Railroad through Santa Fe.

6. **1680** - The revolt of the Pueblo Native Americans and expulsion of the Spanish from New Mexico.

7. **1540** - Francisco Vasquez de Coronado explores the Southwest and the large area called New Mexico.

8. **1850** - A formal Territorial government is established for New Mexico.

9. **1598** - Colonization of New Mexico is begun by Juan de Oñate.

10. **1846** - This is the first year of the U.S.-Mexican War: Governor Manual Armijo flees to safety and General Kearny occupies Santa Fe.

11. **1807** - Zebulon Pike is held prisoner in Santa Fe for trespassing on Spanish Territory.

12. **1821** - Mexico gains independence from Spain.

The correct time line for these important events is:

1. _____	5. _____	9. _____
2. _____	6. _____	10. _____
3. _____	7. _____	11. _____
4. _____	8. _____	12. _____

The answer to this activity is found on page 46.

Four Flags Over New Mexico

A. During the long history of New Mexico there have been four different flags on the pole in Santa Fe, the state's capital. Can you name these countries? Put your answer beside the clues listed below.

1. S - A - N.

2. M - X - C.

3. C - N - E - E - A - E - S - A - E - O - A - E - I - A.

4. U - I - E- S - A - E - O - A - E - I - A.

B. What state once claimed the territory?

1. T - X - S.

The answers to these questions can be found on page 47

You will find four uncompleted flags on the next page. They represent the countries that are the answers to question #1.

Complete these flags using the color key.

Four flags over New Mexico

2.

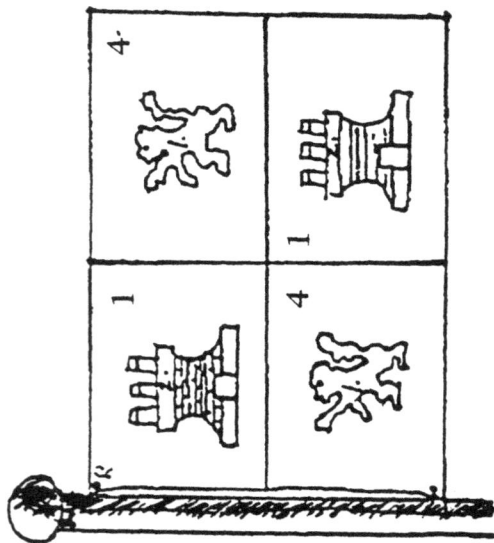

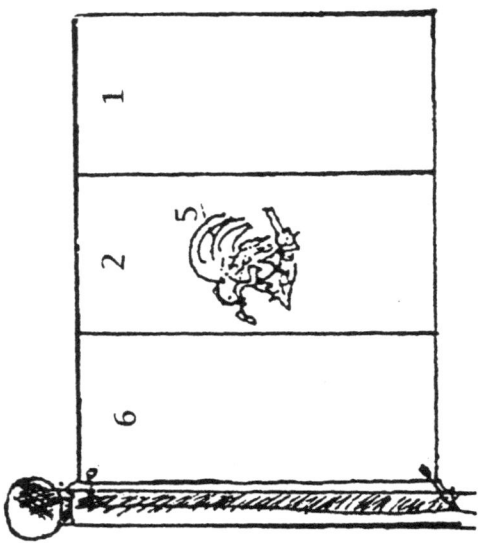

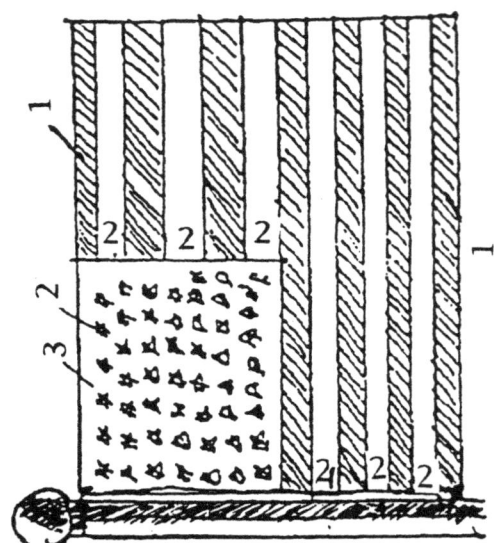

Name of the country _____

4.

Name of the country _____

1.

Name of the country _____

3.

Name of the country _____

Color Key: 1 - red, 2 - white, 3 - Blue, 4 - Yellow, 5 - Brown, 6 - Green.

The Camino Real Mystery Object Challenge

Here are six objects that are associated with the Camino Real. Can you identify what they are called and for what purpose they were used?

To discover the names and uses for these objects turn this page upside down.

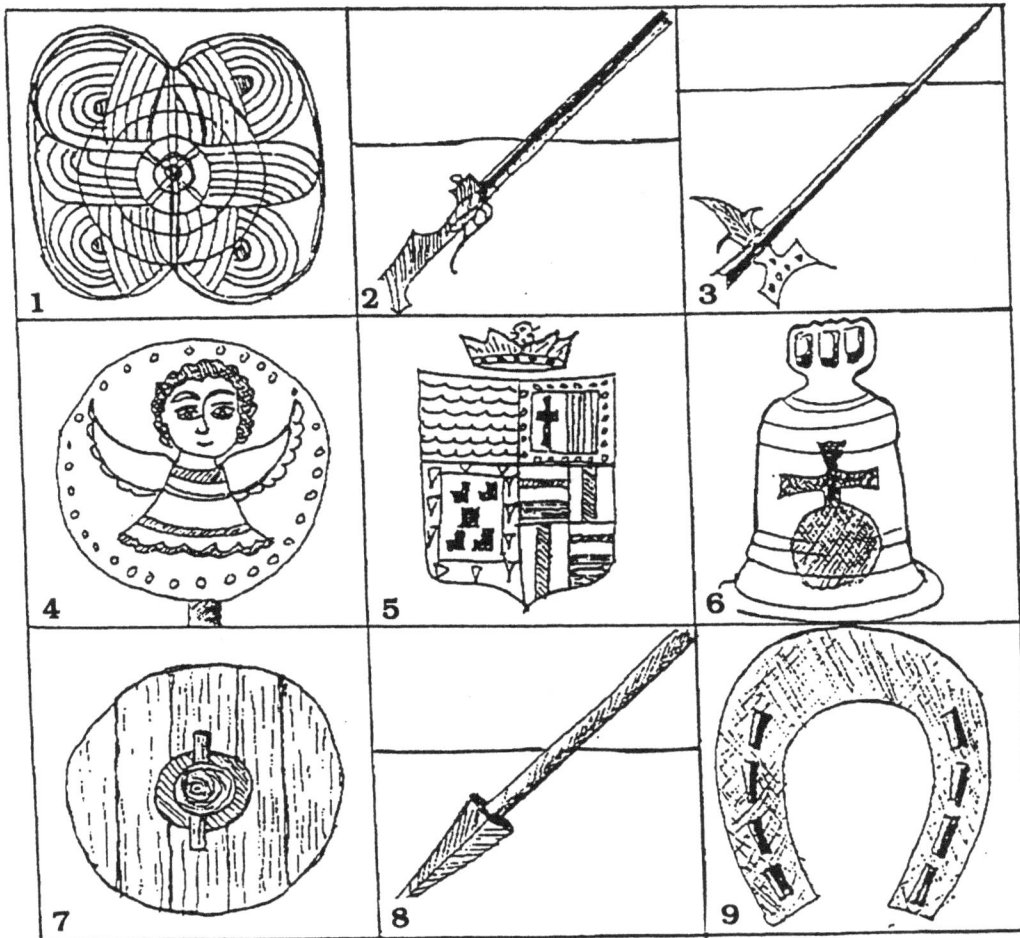

1. Spanish cowhide shield used by officers
2. A Spanish musket (gun) called an escopeta
3. A pike or alabarda commonly used as a weapon
4. A colonial Spanish altar decoration (an angel)
5. An early Spanish coat of arms used to identify a landed family
6. A long waisted cast bronze bell used in Spanish missions
7. An ox cart wheel made of large hand-hewn logs
8. A goad used to prod oxen and cattle to move on
9. A cast iron shoe used for oxen

Fun with cut and color

Here is a page of cut and color figures. Using these drawings as models, create your own scene of the Camino Real. Remember you will need several mules to create an **atajo**. You will find other cut and color pages which will have additional items you will need to compose your scene of the trail.

Oxen

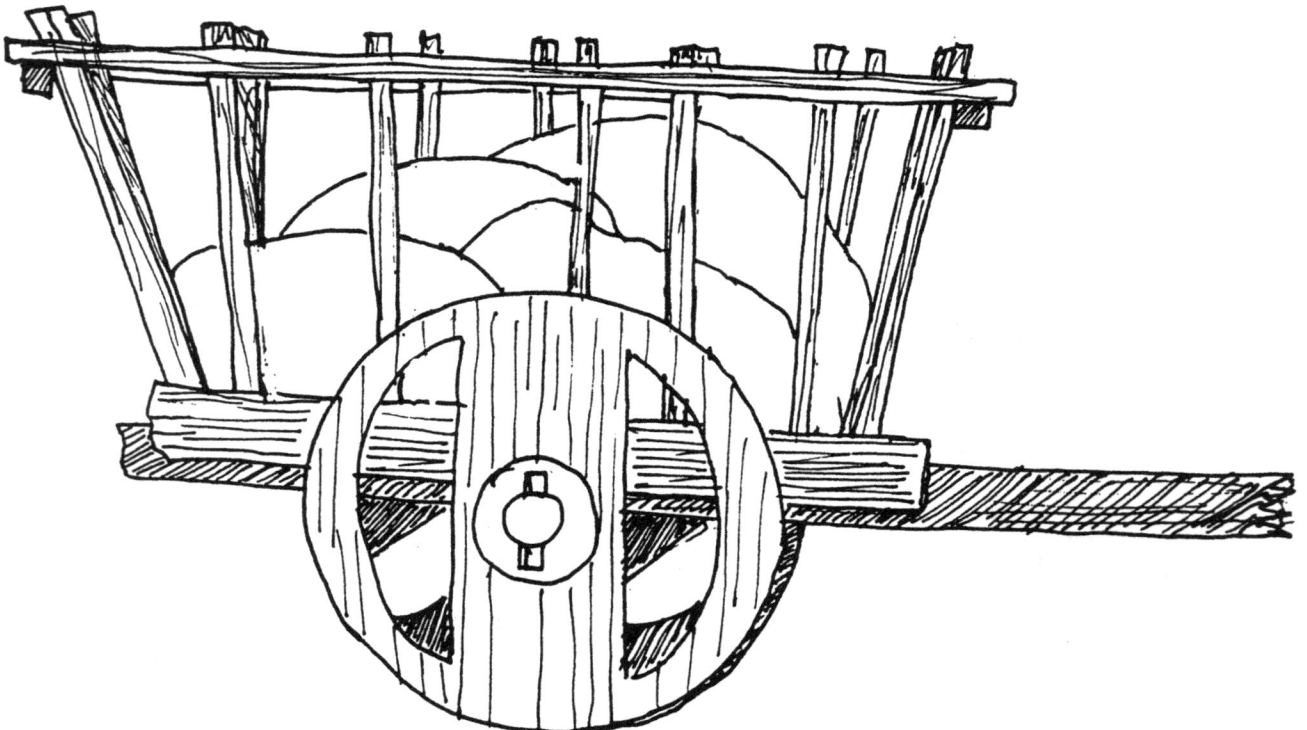

Carreta

Fun with cut and color

Here is a page of cut and color figures. Using these drawings as models create your own scene of the Camino Real. Remember you will need several mules to create an **atajo**. You will find other cut and color pages which will have additional items you will need to compose your scene of the trail.

Pack Mule

Burro

Spanish Soldiers

Spanish Soldiers

Make a model of a **carromato**, a Spanish wagon.

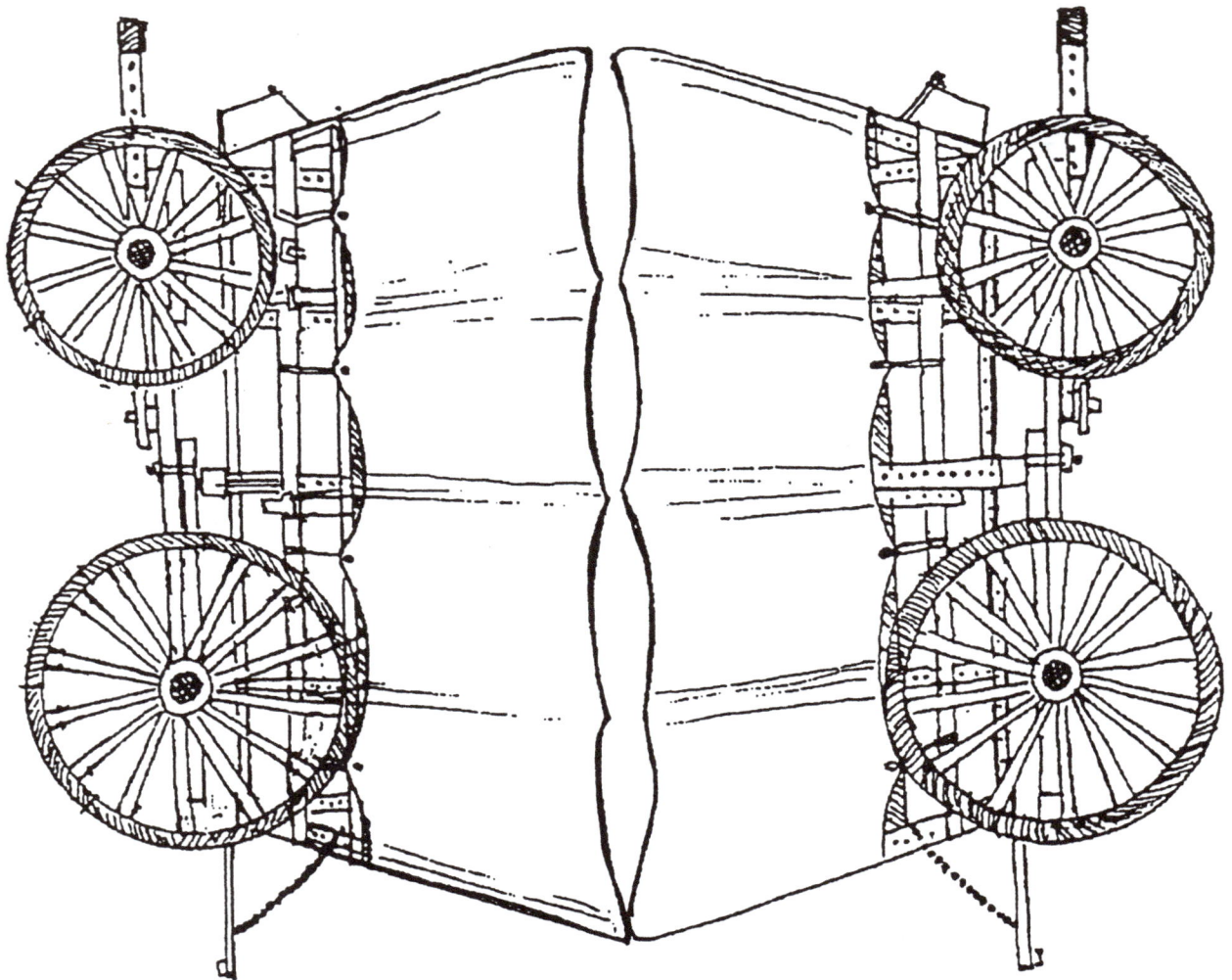

Color the box blue, the undercarriage red and the iron parts black.

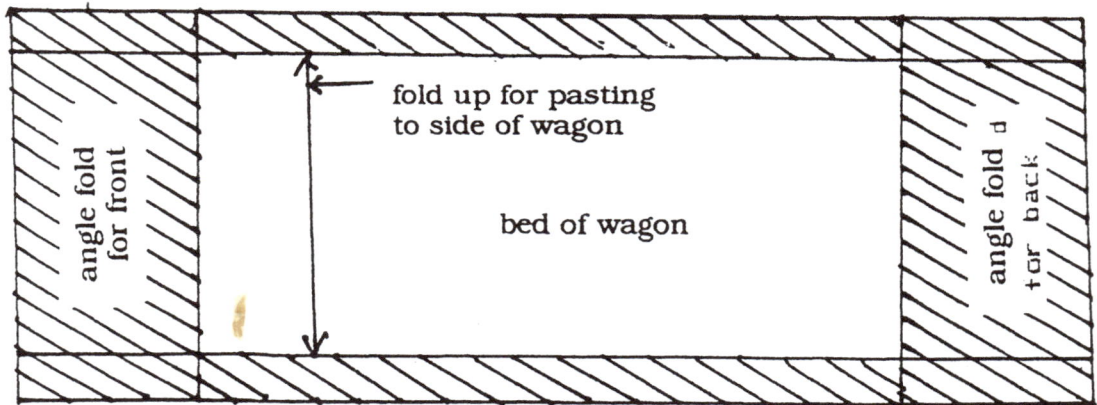

angle fold for front	fold up for pasting to side of wagon	angle fold for back
	bed of wagon	

The Prairie Schooner was not built the same way as a Conestoga Wagon. The cargo box or bed had a flat bottom and was not as large. To complete a model of a Prairie Schooner cut out the two sides of the wagon as shown above and tape or paste them to the box pattern shown at the bottom of the page. It will be easier and more successful if you color or decorate your wagon before putting it together. This type of cargo wagon was used on both the Santa Fe Trail and the Camino Real.

Fun with cut and color

Here is a page of cut and color figures. Using these drawings as models, create your own scene of the Camino Real. Remember you will need several mules to create an **atajo**. You will find other cut and color pages which will have additional items you will need to compose your scene of the trail.

Spanish Foot Soldier

Priest

Mule train Leader

Hispanic Rancher

Mule

A holiday scene to color

Complete these four words by filling the blanks provided.

People living along the Camino Real hold colorful f - e - t - s
Throughout the year. At c - r - s - m - s time a blindfolded person must
break the P - ñ - t- so everyone can share the candy hidden inside. The
dancers wear large hats called s - m - r - r - s.

The answers to this activity can be found on page 47.

Camino Real Famous Person List

Listed below are several important persons to remember that helped develop the Camino Real. Read about each one and complete the crossword puzzle on the next page.

Francisco Vasquez de Coronado - He led the first group of Conquistadores into the area now known as New Mexico in 1540. He searched for the fabled "Seven Cities of Gold" but found out they were only a myth.

Hernando Cortez - He and his small army conquered Mexico in 1521. Less than thirty years later Mexico was being used as a base to explore the unknown regions of the western side of North America.

Don Juan de Oñate - King Philip of Spain gave Oñate the right to colonize the region of New Mexico in 1583. In 1598 he and his group traveled up the Rio Grande to Santa Fe, New Mexico. He established the first capital in Española, New Mexico.

Garcia Lopez de Cardenas - He led a small band of Spanish explorers into northern Arizona in 1540. They were the first white men to see the Colorado River and the Grand Canyon.

Pedro de Peralta - Was the first Royal Governor of New Mexico. He established the capital at Santa Fe in 1610. This is the oldest capital city in the United States.

Gaspar Castaño de Sosa - In 1590 he led a group of Spanish colonists up the Rio Grande from Old Mexico. This group of colonists were the first travelers to use wheeled vehicles on the Camino Real.

Don Diego de Vargas - He was named Governor and Captain General of New Mexico in 1688. He drove the native Americans out of Santa Fe where they had been in power for twelve years. The Pueblo Revolt was over.

Juan Bautista de Anza - He became the Governor of New Mexico in 1778. He defeated Cuerno Verde, known as Green Horn, a Comanche War Chief in 1779. This Comanche leader made peace with the Spanish in 1786.

Augustin de Iturbide - A Mexican General who after several battles against the Spanish Army defeated them and declared Mexico free from Spain. New Mexico became the property of Mexico.

Manuel Armijo - He put down the Chimayo Rebellion and was Governor of New Mexico during the U.S.-Mexican War. He was forced to leave after being defeated by General Kearney. New Mexico became part of the United States in 1848.

Jean B. Lamy - Became the Bishop of New Mexico in 1851. He brought discipline to the church and built forty-five new churches. He become the Archbishop of New Mexico in 1875.

Henry H. Sibley - A Brigadier General who lead 2600 men into New Mexico during the American Civil War. In 1862 he was defeated by the Union Army, under Col. Edward Canby, at the Glorieta Pass near Santa Fe. The Confederate occupation of New Mexico came to an end.

The Camino Real

Famous Person Crossword Puzzle

Complete the crossword puzzle below after reading about these famous leaders on the previous page. There are a few clues to get you started. Take your time. Doing an illustrated report about one or all of these persons would be a great way to learn more about the Camino Real.

The solution to this puzzle is on page 47.

A Colonial Spanish Coat of Arms

People in Spain who own large estates generally have a family coat of arms. They are brightly colored and symbolize power and position granted by the King. The coat of arms below belonged to Diego de Vargas, the Spanish aristocrat, who became the leader of New Mexico in 1691.

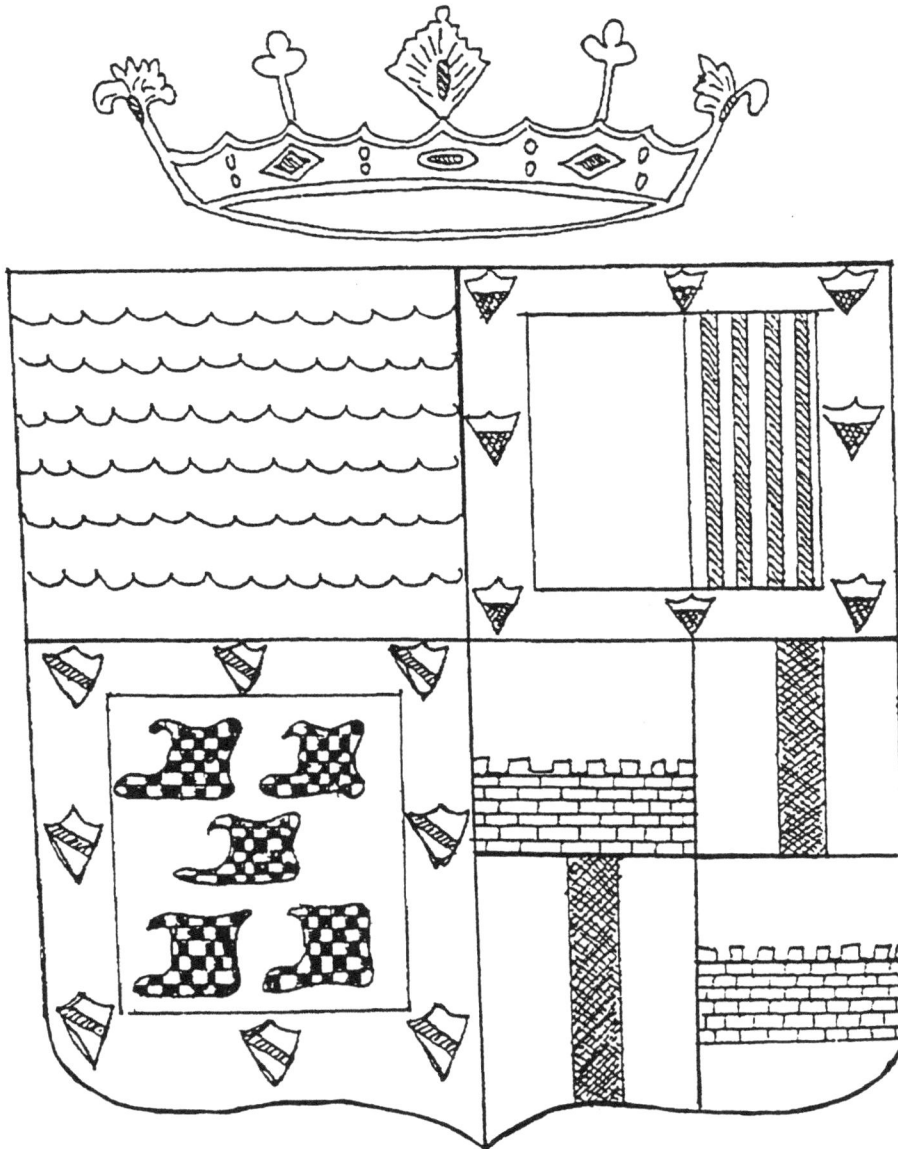

Use bright, pure colors to complete this symbol of power and position

Pick a few favorite objects and design your own family coat of arms.

Create your own " Coat of Arms "

A coat of arms is like a sign you might put on your house, stationery or your shirt pocket. It shows your friends what your are proud of. This might be your family heritage, or a special thing or skill for which you wish to be recognized. For example; if you are an artist you could include items like a brush or a palette on your coat of arms. If you excel at a sport you could include a ball or a bat. You could use your initials. Take your time and make a list of your ideas before you begin.

Complete your " Coat of Arms " by selecting bright colors.

Resting on the Plaza in Old Santa Fe
A Camino Real Scene to Color

Fill in the missing blanks in this description

Santa Fe, New Mexico, was situated at the end of both the Camino Real and the Santa Fe Trail. It was an exciting place full of traders, Native Americans, Anglos, and Hispanics. Parties were held often. These celebrations were called **f - n - a - g - s**. Anglo traders from the east were fascinated with the friendliness of the Santa Feans. There was plenty of night life, they wore bright colors and were fond of music and dancing.

The answer to this activity can be found on page 47.

San Isidro

Since the early inhabitants of New Mexico were chiefly ranchers, sheepmen, and miners, the most popular household saints are San Isidro, patron of farmers and protector of their fields; San Antonio, patron of flocks and finder of straying lambs and lost articles; and Santo Nino de Atoche, patron of miners and healer of the sick. Many households contain images of one or more of these saints, and almost every household has its own tale of especial blessing from its particular saint, or its own idea of the saint's history and origin. San Isidro belongs particularly to Santa Fe, since he is claimed as a native. Consequently, there are many tales of how and why he became a saint. One of them follows.

Isidro was a hard-working, honest rancher on a small tract of land in Agua Fria on the Rio de Santa Fe, on the outskirts of Santa Fe itself. One year he found himself behind with his plowing. Grass was eating up his crop, and the ground was caking with dryness. So when Sunday morning came, his wife could not persuade him to go to church as usual. Instead , he hitched his two oxen to his plow and began to till his field. Neighbors chided him as they passed.

" The corn will grow and the corn will die, if you plow on Sunday," said one.

" Someday you will be plowing for the devil," suggested another.

But paying no attention to the chiding, Isidro went on with his plowing. The sunshine beat hot upon his head, and perspiration streamed into his mustachio, but he paid no heed to these discomforts.

At length, God Himself, in the form of a man, came to Isidro's field.

" Why are you working on the Lord's Day? " He asked.

Without pausing, Isidro pressed his plow deeper into the stiff adobe and answered, " because my field needs plowing right away. Otherwise my corn and beans will not grow to feed my family." With an impatient gesture, he tried to rid himself of this intruder. " It's easy to go to church, but it's hard to plow for one's family."

" This is the day for prayer," warned the Stranger. " You should be attending Mass in the church. If you desecrate the Sabbath Day, God will send rain to flood your field and destroy your crops."

San Isidro continued.

" From now on I am God. Let the rains come, foolish man. They cannot harm me," boasted Isidro, wiping the sweat from his brow on a tattered sleeve.

" Then," said the Stranger, keeping pace with Isidro, " God will send a scourge of grasshoppers to eat up your crops."

" I am not afraid of grasshoppers. From now on I am God, " again boasted Isidro.

" Well then, God will send a drought to dry up your beans and corn," the Stranger warned him.

" Drought cannot hurt me, for I tell you, from now on I am God."

" Very well then," said the Stranger , " God will send you a bad neighbor. His animals will break into your field and eat up your corn; his dog will bite you; he will gossip about you to his neighbors; and he will take away your wife. God will send a bad neighbor."

" Lord have mercy upon me!" cried Isidro, quickly unhitching his oxen from the plow. " May God not punish me with a bad neighbor! I must go pray."

Forgetting to stall his oxen, ignoring the stranger, and unmindful of his clothes, Isidro ran down the road, stumbling over its ruts and stones and winding with it as the roadway traced the distinct dividing line between narrow, long ranches on the river-side and the vast green-dotted carpet of eroded land. where goats browsed, leading up to the Sangre de Cristo Mountains. At last, jerking off his ragged hat, he breathlessly stumbled his way into church, not stopping until he found his wife kneeling before the image of her favorite saint. Humbly he reached for her rosary and began to recite his beads.

When the people came from church, they saw a strange sight in Isidro's field; an angel was driving Isidro's oxen and plowing his field. Thereafter Isidro became a pious and good man, so that later he was made a saint. Today his image is shown as a hatted man, dressed in his Sunday best, walking beside an angel, who is driving two small oxen before a plow.

And this is one of the legends that the people of Santa Fe hear as the bells ring out at the little church in Agua Fria.

San Isidro, The Saint of Farmers

A bulto to color.

Bultos are statues carved from wood and displayed in the home and church to honor respected religious saints and figures. Bultos can be seen in the art and history museums in the Southwest.

Complete this illustration of an angel helping San Isidro using bright colors.

Unloading trade goods from Old Mexico

A Camino Real trail scene to color.

All kinds of wonderful things were brought from both the cities of the Eastern United States and commercial centers of Old Mexico. Many weeks were required to transport items over the Camino Real. Metal items such as plow points, guns and nails were important to the area's farmers. Cooking utensils and fancy dry goods were appreciated by the hard working housewives. Lastly, a few fortunate boys and girls were able to acquire toys and games from foreign lands. The Camino Real enabled traders to bring goods both north and south through New Mexico Territory along the Rio Grande River.

Complete this trail trading scene using colors suggested by the objects in the picture.

Luxuries* Come to La Madera

A small community near Las Placitas, New Mexico

It was in the late 1870s that the last teams of oxen and wagons left La Madera for Kansas City and Old Mexico, those great markets at the eastern and southern ends of the Camino Real. It was with unusual excitement that preparations for the six month trip were undertaken. But it was not the trip or the preparation for it that was the big event this time: it was the happy home-coming of **Señor*** Rumaldo Candelario who had made several trips before this one for his **Patron*,** taking wool to market and bringing back precious cargoes of merchandise. He had always gone with empty pockets. This trip he had some money of his own to spend. He had brought back goods like those bought for his Patron. When he arrived with his treasure, his neighbors crowded about his door to see what he had brought. They looked on breathless as he unwrapped the bundle. There was a whole bolt of **muselina*** and two large copper kettles! And the last and most glorious of all was a bolt of **Calico!*** At the sight of that, the women opened their eyes in surprise and sighed aloud with pleasure. What a present for Rumaldo to bring home to his wife and daughters! **Senõra*** Candelario could scarcely believe the evidence of her eyes. When she was a girl, calico brought over the trail from Kansas City sold for ten dollars a yard in Santa Fe. Even now it was so expensive that only the rich could afford to buy it. And the snowy white muselina! The first bride of the family should have a dress and veil of it.

And that first bride did wear a dress and veil of it. The veil was fastened to her hair at one side of her head and had wild flowers pinned on it where it touched her skirt, as well as where it was fastened to her hair. This dress and veil were borrowed and worn by other brides who preferred them to the **Merino*** outfits woven at home from the wool of their goats.

Luxuries - Something desirable but costly and hard to get.
Senor - Mister in Spanish
Patron - Is the owner of the land on which Rumaldo lived.
Muselina - Is Spanish for muslin, a plain woven cotton fabric.
Calico - Is a finely woven cotton fabric originally from India
Senora - Is the lady of the house, the wife of Rumaldo
Merino - This is a coarse wool taken from goats or sheep

The information above was excerpted from a story told by Rumaldita Gurule to Lou Sage Batchen of Placitas, New Mexico.

A mirror image challenge

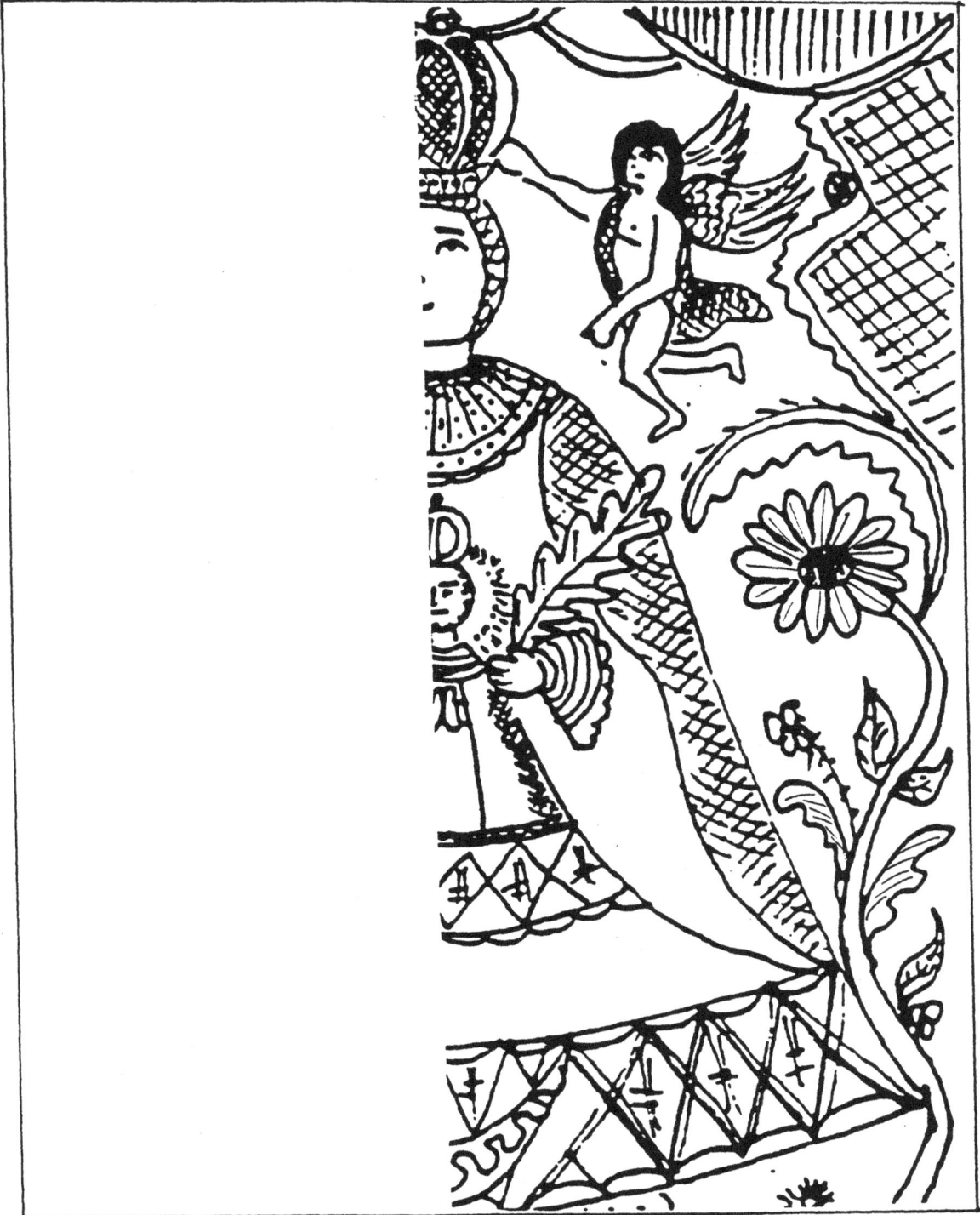

This is a retablo or religious picture of Mother Mary and baby Jesus. This is an important symbol found in all Christian religions. Both sides of the retablo are identical. See if you can complete the unfinished half. Use a pencil so you can erase any mistakes.

Complete this retablo by using bright hot and cold colors.

A Symbol for the Camino Real

A Design to Color

This symbol using the Native American Zia sun symbol and a team of oxen pulling a wooden carreta was designed to mark important places along the present day Camino Real. Should you travel from Santa Fe, New Mexico to El Paso, Texas, look for these signs along the way.

Fill in the areas of this symbol with the colors shown in the color key.

Color Key
1. black
2. turquoise blue
3. dark yellow
4. vivid pink
5. areas in shadow are black

A Dedication to Our Friend the Burro

(or the Donkey)

It has been said that there was no town in the West that had more burros than Santa Fe, New Mexico. For over three hundred years the burro was the main means of transportation in the southwestern regions of North America. No other beast of burden did more work than this nimble little animal. This sure footed friend of man was the bearer of wood, water, trunks, alfalfa, boxes, and thousands of wiggley children. The burro served as the comunity alarm clock by braying at the crack of dawn. The loud 'hee-aw, hee-aw' could be heard for a great distance. The burro or donkey has not been a common sight for many years. This dedicated animal is honored for the hard working support it gave to the history and progress of the Southwest.

A Santo to Color

A Santo is a picture of a Saint or religious figure. These pictures were used to teach people about the Catholic Church. Bright colors were used to finish these unique and historic symbols of the Church. Many of these original Santos can be seen in museums and old village missions and churches of New Mexico.

Some parts of this Santo are missing. Both halves of the picture are almost exactly the same. Fill in the missing parts and complete the Santo with bright colors.

An Early New Mexico Retablo Design To Color

Pictures such as this were found in the Missions, Chapels, and Churches of early New Mexico. Today many of these religious retablos and santos are found in museums and are very valuable. Bright colors are used to complete these religious pictures.

The Camino Real Modern Town Word Search

Listed below are many towns, cities and villages that have grown up on the ancient route of the Camino Real. Many of these settlements are directly on the trail while others are very near the trail. You can locate these current cities by checking your state map. Put a check mark by the towns that are directly on the Camino Real. Remember that the words can be horizontal, vertical, diagonal, or even backwards.

```
N O V X Y O F A B M C H O L L A B A C D F G H S
C R O T B A L A M E D A E I P J O K Q L M N L G
D E R R Y P O N O S H T L O S P A D I L L A S N
M E L A S I R B R I Z C O P M N O V R S M T Z I
E Z V H W V I X Y L Z H H E B M N N O E V H E R
S X Y Q E P D Z H L A S C R U C E S S R S M V P
Q U E R M O A K L A I V O A H N L A Y V V Z X S
U S U T O N Y J M I M B B L V V E O B M C N O M
I O Q P T N L M A B E N R T Q I B P E V H H O U
T S S H U O E J X R Z H L A S N U T R I A S M I
E A O P R W M H I N I V U N I O N V N E M M I D
N N B Q N R T N O C S T L L O Z I M A H B R Z A
Y A W A S U O G A R T F O A P M V N L V E A E R
E N R Y V T R N Q E E Y S S O M E L I B R F V O
R T N O N V U B L U Z V L P L O R O L F I E A E
A O A J M T O G B D W A U A V N S P L B N U H D
A I O L S E N O D O G L A O R M T S Z A G S S S
G O L V Q L P C O S A Z S M E S Y Y L W X O O R
R O B W U E L N N R R Y I A D U P V H E B B L T
U X E E S P E I M A F O C S A T A I K J T O P O
B I R F B H M R V L I S O N C O R R O L M N A W Y
S L N A D A I A L O E E N H A M K O B H Z V X M
M I A T G N T O Z H L I T O V L A C I E N A G A
A S R N R T A B Y E D U E H O E A B Z H O O V E
I J D A D B R A Y S R Q R V B M G B H M L M X Y
L G O S E U D O N A A N A P N O M U N H O V P O
L K X L B T O L Y L U I S L O P E Z I B M L Q U
I M O A F T B O Z A T S X U V W O B X T M O S R
W L Y Z H E N M H B E U Q R E U Q U B L A N J V
```

Santa Fe
Alameda
Isleta
Tome
Turn
Florida
Engle
Las Palomas
Garfield
Radium Springs
Mesilla
Chamberino

La Cienaga
Albuquerque
Bosque Farms
Los Chaves
Veguita
LaJoya
Luis Lopez
Elephant Butte
Caballo
Salem
Dona Ana
Mesquite
Union

Bernalillo
Los Padillas
Los Lunas
Bosque
Bernardo
Lemitar
San Antonio
T ot C
Derry
Hatch
University Park
Berino
Anthony

Algodones
Pajarito
Peralta
Belen
Las Nutrias
Polvareda
Socorro
Williamsburg
Arrey
Rincon
Las Cruces
La Mesa
Canutillo

The solution to this word search is on page 47.

A Spanish Barb With a Military Rider

The horse (or el caballo) was brought to western America by the Spaniards. These strong and swift animals descended from a breed of African horses called Barbs. These horses were developed by the ancient Romans and by the Moors of Spain. Horses brought to the Rio Grande valley roamed free in large herds and some went wild.
The horses were called M _ S _ A _ _ S.

The Spanish name for a saddle horse is *caballo de silla.*

The answer to this question can be found on page 47.

Answer page

From page 5 - 1. Utah
2. Colorado
3. Kansas
4. Oklahoma
5. Texas
6. New Mexico
7. Arizona
8. Mexico

From page 7 - Word search solution.

From page 9 - A - 4, B - 1, C - 3, D - 2, E - 5,
From page 10 - 1. Is a very large desert.
2. is a group of large and extensive sand dunes.
3. Is a long route with no water.
From page 11 1. Frozen vegetables
2. Radios
3. Electric razors
4. Canned Fruit
5. Ice cream
From page 13 - The correct date is 1590 A.D.
From page 15 - List #1 are goods going south to Mexico
List #2 are goods going north is Santa Fe.
From page 16 - The Mystery object is a torreon or tower.
From page 20 - 7, 9, 6, 4, 11, 12, 3, 10, 8, 2, 5, 1.

From page 21 - **(A)** 1. Spain
2. Mexico
3. The Confederate States of America
4. The United States of America

(B) Texas

From page 28 - Fiesta, Christmas, Piñata, Sombreros.

From page 30 - Crossword puzzle solution.

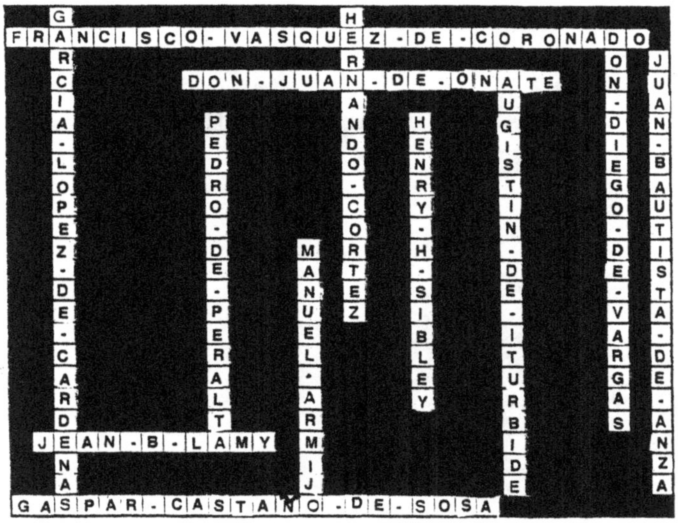

From page 44 - Word Search solution.

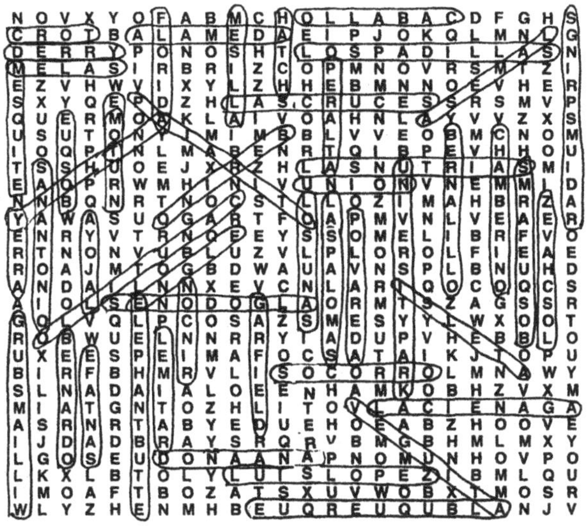

From page 33 - Fandangos

From page 45 - Mustangs

Credits and bibliography

DeHuff, Elizabeth Willis, Say the Bells of Old Missions, B. Herder Book Co., St. Louis, 1943. Pages 131 - 134.

Batchen, Sage Lou, Las Placitas, Historcal Facts and Legends, Tumble Weed Press, Placitas New Mexico, 1972, Pages 84, 85, and 90.

Adams, Samuel Hopkins, The Santa Fe Trail, Random House, New York, 1951.

Many thanks to the staff of Zimmerman Library, Center for Southwest Research, Bonnie J. Yoder, Editor and the many teachers of the Albuquerque Public School System who assisted in the field testing of this book.

www.ingramcontent.com/pod-product-compliance
Lightning Source LLC
Chambersburg PA
CBHW081420090426
42738CB00017B/3431